BOA
EDITIONS
LIMITED

12-31-87

Merry Christmas Poppa—
until I read these
small verses did it
even exist in English—
Ital Translation!
"When a spring wind
touches me,
alone, I'll take my
boat across."

love,
S + S

SONGS
OF
THE
KISAENG

Courtesan Poetry
of the Last Korean Dynasty

Translated and Introduced by
CONSTANTINE CONTOGENIS
AND
WOLHEE CHOE

Drawings by
WONSOOK KIM

BOA Editions, Ltd. ❧ Rochester, NY ❧ 1997

LC #: 96–80160
ISBN 1–880238–53–5 paper

First Edition
97 98 99 00   7 6 5 4 3 2 1

This publication was made possible by a grant from
The Korean Culture & Arts Foundation.
Publications by BOA Editions, Ltd.—a not-for-profit corporation
under section 501 (c) (3) of the United States Internal Revenue Code—
are supported by grants from
the Literature Program of the New York State Council on the Arts,
the Literature Program of the National Endowment for the Arts,
the Lannan Foundation, the Sonia Raiziss Giop Charitable Foundation,
the Eric Mathieu King Fund of The Academy of American Poets,
as well as from the Rochester Area Foundation Community Arts Fund
administered by the Arts & Cultural Council for Greater Rochester,
the County of Monroe, NY,
and from many individual supporters.

Cover Design: Geri McCormick
Cover painting and text drawings by Wonsook Kim
Typesetting: Richard Foerster
Printed in Canada by Best Book Manufacturers
BOA Logo: Mirko

BOA Editions, Ltd.
Alexandra Northrop, Chair
A. Poulin, Jr., Founder and President (1976-1996)
260 East Avenue
Rochester, NY 14604

SONGS
OF
THE
KISAENG

Courtesan Poetry
of the Last Korean Dynasty

Contents

Introduction

I. The Identity of the Kisaeng

The poems translated here as *Songs of the Kisaeng* were written primarily in the sixteenth and seventeenth centuries by an unusual group of Korean women called kisaeng, who were a combination of professional entertainer, performing artist, and courtesan. A few poems in the collection were sung by kisaeng from the fifteenth through the eighteenth century, when they were collected and written down. The kisaeng (sometimes called "skilled women") were selected from the lower classes for their beauty, youth, and talent and were forced to work for what was, in effect, the government performing-arts bureaucracy. A number of the kisaeng wrote with a rare blend of emotional freedom, ironic perspective, and technical mastery, which enabled them, with fewer than a hundred poems, to establish an enduring tradition of love poetry.

A kisaeng's creative performance in music and dance was of the moment only, not considered worthy to be part of the officially recorded culture of her time. Even her less ephemeral artistic expressions, her poems, survived only against the odds. Those that did survive were passed on orally or through private collections before they were compiled into anthologies by scholars, often, it seems, a century or more after the death of the poet. These poems survived initially because of the personal (as contrasted with scholarly) concern of individuals. Therefore, the lack of precise dates for the poems and their poets is the rule. Yet it is possible to place them historically, albeit very roughly. Some historical information has been gained about these poems through references to them made by the company the kisaeng kept. That the poems were kept alive at all, against the overwhelming odds established by Confucian ideology, attests to their strength and the poetic genius of these women.

A number of the kisaeng, who lived as quasi-persons, are known to us today as women of strong identities—that is, as woman poets. Although placed near the periphery of Korean society, these kisaeng poets managed, paradoxically, to reposition themselves to the center of Korean culture. How was this achievement possible?

Let us consider some of the personal details from the common lot of the kisaeng. A kisaeng was taken away from her family and schooled for a career that prevented her from having a normal marriage and family. However, she had more economic independence than other women of her time and freedom to associate with men of power and learning. To a significant extent, she could become her own person, able to cultivate her identity through her skills. She could not help knowing the lowly person she was socially, of course, but her dance, her music, and her poetry enabled her to define her unique personality, with few upper limits on her sophistication, learning, or general cultivation.

The primary audience for the kisaeng-performers was the king (and, occasionally, the queen). The secondary audience was exclusively male and included the prime minister, provincial governors, the powerful class of scholar-bureaucrats (poets, painters, calligraphers), idle aristocrats, and foreign envoys. Soldiers were also included, both the aristocratic officers and the more common rank and file. Placements for the kisaeng ranged from the royal palace, where they might perform refined rituals at feasts of greeting and farewell to the king, to border guard military posts, where their principle role was probably sexual.[1]

A kisaeng's paradoxical identity as a socially despised yet popularly (unofficially) acclaimed artist in music, dance, and, at times, poetry may well have given her the kind of sustained self-consciousness necessary to the search for a unique identity. Through reflections on her disciplined exertions and on her separate status, she would have been able to attain a sense also of the boundaries of selfhood. Her skills established her individuality by allowing her to exist within a culture in her own way. Her personality was given birth and survived by being identified with the way she used her skills—that is, with her style.

Those kisaeng who wrote the poems in this volume were thus allowed to be more "themselves" than most other women of the time. This is not to suggest that the house bound pains and pleasures of other Korean women during the Chosun Dynasty (1392–1910) were somehow less their own; the point is, rather, that the Confucian social order had effectively denied women a legitimate medium for expressing their experiences and feelings in their own way. Although lower-class women were somewhat freer, Korean women in general, who had feminine "virtues" stringently imposed on them, were denied almost any skill (other than for pure physical labor or household tasks) and were thereby denied the most developed, accomplished, and refined form of themselves. The kisaeng, however, were allowed the means to be articulate and to become more fully human than even their female social superiors. It is in this context that these collected kisaeng poems may help suggest some ways of understanding the interrelations between selfhood and creativity.

As an artist, a kisaeng remained anonymous. However skilled and accomplished her poetic compositions were, they could not bring to her any societal or official acknowledgment in her lifetime. Neither did they bring any change to the existing social system. The highest recognition she could receive was a reputation among the men she entertained, which might have brought some attendant increase in work and financial comfort. But she could never attain sufficient standing as an author in her time to have her essential biographical data recorded. Yet the kisaeng poets' influence on the lyrical tradition of Korean poetry and on popular culture is indelible.

What can we conjecture about the current appeal of kisaeng poetry? Can a contemporary American woman compare herself to a kisaeng? Despite their emergence from widely differing cultures and histories, one cannot help noting a certain ambiguity that is creatively endured by both groups of women. For instance, a kisaeng's skills and her freedom from many "feminine" social rules allowed her to develop her own personality. In much the same way, a "postmodern" American woman, responding to the collapsing models of femininity, often develops her sense of identity based more on talents and skills than on socially imposed roles. Both women may come to an appreciation of a self founded on a creative life rather than on a life created for them.

The great differences between the women of such different eras and traditions are of course easier to note. The creative life of the kisaeng was linked with her social degradation, whereas, today, it is no longer necessary for women to enter the demimonde to achieve self-expression. When a kisaeng excelled in poetic achievement, her authorship was often ignored because of her insubstantial social status. By contrast, an American woman today has a social position close to that of men, albeit often without commensurate economic power.

Still, one of the simplest and most cogent reasons for the current interest in the kisaeng poems is more than political. The kisaeng left us good, moving poems with a direct and timeless lyrical voice. By contrast, many of the poems written by men of the Chosun Dynasty are historical, topical, and thus, not as accessible to the contemporary reader.

A kisaeng's poem can make the difficulties of her life seem universal, and actually enables the reader to experience some of the same problems. For instance, the problem of securely placing oneself within a shattered social and emotional context is as much a problem now, in the west, as it was several hundred years ago for the kisaeng. For another, her profession, which demanded her infidelity (and the infidelity of respectably married male bureaucrats), ironically defines a universal condition of romantic love, for a kisaeng in love is a lover obsessed with abandonment. A kisaeng must have been prepared to abandon her lover physically for the male participants of the next feast she was summoned to. She must also have been prepared to see her lover abandon her in the future, to recognize that her lover had abandoned her, indeed, to understand that her lover, in a sense, had always abandoned her.

It is easy to imagine that the typical encounter between kisaeng and guest was contingent upon, or defined within, the limits of infidelity and abandonment. In this context, it was as though an experiment in love were being conducted by the kisaeng. The usual elements of exclusivity, permanence, and vowing are "factored out" to see what's left as part of love. The very act of vowing is used by these kisaeng poets to uncover the confusion in the notion that exclusivity and permanence are part of love. That is, if love "naturally" includes vowing, it can not "naturally" include exclusivity or permanence. If vowing is necessary, exclusivity is not automatic. The notion that love is purely natural (whatever else it may be) is also effectively questioned. Artifice and art are both seen to be essential ingredients. An anonymous kisaeng poem from the seventeenth century illustrates some of this analysis of the state of loving:

> An anchor lifts, a ship is leaving.
> He goes this time, when to return.
> Far over the sea's vast waverings
> one can see a going as return.

> But at the sound of that anchor lifting,
> the night could feel her insides turn.

In this poem, the universal theme of abandonment in love is developed through a narration, partly biological, social, and emotional, of a kisaeng who is parting with her lover, perhaps a lover of one night. She sings of the lover's absence in terms of the ordeal of parting, waiting, and despair. A lover visits and departs, a permanent relationship does not exist. In a kisaeng's life this fact, which few women willingly espouse, is accepted as a matter of course. However, this does not negate her love, which, like postmodern love, is assumed to be precarious. Her song also affirms a love that, although in part a delusion, is an authentic reality, an artistic achievement: "Far over the sea's vast waverings/ one can see a going as return." This created reality, this artificial aspect of love is finally seen (in the identification with the night: "the night could feel her insides turn") as part of the natural order and the "natural" state of love.

A kisaeng could sometimes talk (and write) as an intellectual equal to the men she served. Although stigmatized by her Confucian culture because of her knowledge and never considered socially respectable, she could be respected by individuals and as an individual, even loved and longed for by scholar-poets. There are legendary love stories about kisaeng and famous men of the time. The greatest poet in our collection is Hwang Jini (1511?–1541?), whose fame reached a mythic status soon after her death and continues to fascinate Koreans. She is supposed to have had a number of famous lovers, among them, a sage, a scholar, and a young man who, the legend says, died of his love for her and during his own funeral procession refused to move from her doorstep until graced with some of her undergarments for his trip to the grave. Im Je (1549–1587), a respected scholar-poet, left a tribute to her in sijo form, which gives a small measure of her great influence:

> Are you napping or just hiding, lying
> still in this gully of wild blue grass?
> Where is the high color of your face?
> Only white bones lie here.
>
> I hold a cup you can never fill
> that I cannot raise to my sorrow.

Since Confucianism demanded women's absolute faithfulness to one man, the more thoughtful kisaeng are likely to have lived in moral conflict;

even the most obtuse may have felt the pain of separation from all women not of their special institution. A condition of the survival of the kisaeng's moral sense would then likely be her forgetfulness of Confucian edicts. This condition may have helped, ironically, to strengthen her love poems by freeing her from the emotional and expressive constraints of Confucianism. On an important level, she sings of the strength of her loving, loving better than she is loved (Hwang Jini, "Whenever Did I"), loving a man less trustworthy than a sea gull (Hongjang, "Under the Cold, Pine Arbor Moon"). But on a more fundamental level, these are surely audacious poems. A kisaeng is professionally unable to give her own word or to pledge trust. Given that the strength of her lyric voice vitiates accusations of her own hypocrisy, what principles allow her to complain, albeit with resignation, of others? What secret has she discovered about the intensities of love that takes her beyond the common order of lies and betrayals? A kisaeng was, as mentioned, a professional betrayer, and yet some of them developed a genuine sense of betrayal that had nothing to do with exclusivity or permanence. These kisaeng poems suggest that our casual contemporary knowledge of love is not secure; our understanding is incomplete.

Another salient feature which gives characteristic shape to these poems, grown on the fringe of society, is a proudly defiant sense of humor. Songi, whose name literally translates as "pine-female person," sees herself as a special pine tree.

> So, you can tell I'm a pine,
> but what kind do you take me for?
> I've grown tall and wide
> overlooking this precipice.
>
> And you, prentice, from below the timber
> road, wish a pruning blade on me.

She places herself above her work and crowd; she refuses to bend herself, at least, her sense of herself, to meet the common demands on a kisaeng. She chooses her lovers, though perhaps not her clients, as a poet chooses her words. Even when she complains about a lover, she is precisely defiant toward him, but much more interestingly, also defiant toward herself.

Everything you do, everything
you don't do, deceives.
When I love, I make you
my enemy.

But the words you spoke
keep themselves within me.

Given such a complex sense of self and her relative freedom from the rigid codes of her society, she was able to maneuver her life through the conflicting norms her culture set up. Though rooted in and resigned to her social position, her poems show a sense of emotional freedom seemingly unbounded by her place and time. A kisaeng's status as an outsider gave her a privileged position from which to observe and reflect on life. Characteristically silent about historical events, institutions, and ideologies, she projects, instead, an image of a woman who is disciplined against the values of sentimentality but also disciplined to recognize and cherish authentic sentiment within herself.

II. Historical Perspective

There is a good deal of historical information available about the institution of the kisaeng. The kisaeng were the only consistently well-educated group of women throughout Korean history, up until the early twentieth century. An elaborate system of schooling and training was established for them, replete with academic rewards and punishments, on a variety of subjects and levels. Individual achievement varied greatly, of course, and so did official educational policy toward the kisaeng over the 500-year course of the Chosun Dynasty. In all probability, though, among the kisaeng, almost regardless of the period, literacy was universal, and advanced knowledge of literature, social manners, and ritual music and dance was common. Further specialization was often possible for the apt or obedient in such areas as music, medicine, needlework, and, informally, prostitution.[2]

As a marginal woman, however, the kisaeng had to live in a situation painfully unfit for ordinary respectability. To understand her social position, it is necessary to compare it to that of other Korean women. In the Chosun

Dynasty, during which all the poems in this collection were written, women (especially of the upper class) were effectively incarcerated during daylight and, even at home, were forbidden direct contact with any man outside the family. If, for example, a husband were away and his visiting friend were to find the wife alone, she would be obliged to use an indirect form of address, openly pretending to direct an imaginary maid to inform the guest of her husband's whereabouts. Within the family, too, contact between the sexes was severely limited. Furthermore, for the women of the upper class, "doing" often carried the stigma of *having to do*, the stigma of necessity. But for almost any woman, the training she received was rigidly limited to only the most essential tasks of a practical home or farm life. Formal schooling was not provided. Book learning for a woman was discouraged and disparaged.

Confucianism advocated strict hierarchy throughout society, within the family, and between ages and sexes. Its patriarchal system of values extolled rationality and regarded emotional attachment and expression as weaknesses and threats to the social order. While a man who could afford it was expected to marry the woman chosen for him, and have secondary wives or mistresses whom he could choose for himself, it was demanded that once a woman married, she remain sexually and emotionally loyal to her husband during and after his lifetime. She was forbidden even to express jealousy and could be divorced if she did. Acceding to the Confucian ideal of feminine "virtue" resulted in near-helplessness outside a mandated physical and emotional confinement. Individuality for women didn't issue from personal accomplishment so much as from class, gender, and family. In fact, women often lived with only a family name, that is, without a name of their own, without a formal individual identity.

A respectable woman's family name, though unchanged after she married, had only a generic significance by virtue of her presumably selfless devotion to her family. Although her place in her new family as a wife and mother was supposed to be honored and respected, the "virtue" of selflessness made most conceptions of her self-identity logically impossible. This putative honor and respect conferred on her provided no terms for defining her as a separate being. (In fact, the mistreatment of the daughter-in-law is famous throughout Korean folklore.) The higher the honor and the greater the respect, the more conceptual, abstract, and remote became the identity of her person. The denial of skills necessary to survive outside her family meant a denial, to the traditional woman, of the means to survive as a fully developed and unique personality.

By contrast, a kisaeng could address any man directly and provide the intellectual and emotional companionship that "virtuous" wives could not. Thus they became models of women who had interesting lives and exciting personalities. They were given a freedom of social contact between the sexes and a measure of economic independence that were denied to other women. Given this social freedom, the kisaeng were not forced into the usual hypocrisies and false pretenses in matters of affection. A kisaeng might, of course, pretend affection toward anyone, but she was free of the "virtuous" demand that her affection appear to be held for one man (whom she had no part in choosing) throughout her life. She might also pretend, as a good Confucian should, that she experienced no passion, but she was uniquely free, if she chose, to sing of all the passion she could undergo.

One can sense the centrality of the role that the kisaeng institution played within the Chosun Dynasty when noticing that conflicts about the size and maintenance of the institution engaged many of the important political (often in ethical or religious guise), military, and economic concerns of the dynasty. A few historical examples will follow.

During the dynasty, the number of kisaeng employed by the government (with an official stipend of rice) changed dramatically, depending on the particular regime. In the early part of the dynasty, approximately a hundred kisaeng were recruited every third year and sent to the royal court. A similar number of kisaeng were sent, after training, to provincial capitals and military outposts. There were probably a much larger number of unofficial kisaeng throughout the country. But during the reign of Yunsangun (1494–1506), the number of kisaeng in the capital alone reached over 10,000 and were divided into over one hundred specialized categories. The highest category comprised those who were part of the king's household and those formally assigned to the king's bedchamber. Informally, Yunsangun indulged himself with almost any woman or girl taken by his "women hunters." His regime became a focus of many of the debates about the institution and an illustration of the ways in which these debates often reflected larger political issues.[3]

The conflict between religious institutions erupted in Yunsangun's time out of the question of kisaeng housing. Himself a usurper, Yunsangun chose, as part of his consolidation of power through Confucian bureaucrats and away from Buddhist rivals, to house kisaeng by expelling the monks at Wongaksa, the most influential Buddhist monastery of the previous dynasty.[4] The Chosun Dynasty, which had adopted Confucianism as its official religion, had already begun persecuting Buddhists in many subtle ways, but this insult brought the religious and political conflicts of the era into the open.

Yunsangun's sexual abuse of power—nearly bankrupting the state treasury—rivaled those in stories of some of the Roman emperors. This produced controversies, in his and subsequent regimes, about the kisaeng institution, which were, in part, covert debates about the nature, extent, and holders of government power. A faction might oppose the kisaeng institution to oppose the power of the new Confucian bureaucracy, for the bureaucracy was the major recipient of the kisaeng's services. A group might oppose the institution because it depleted the government's funds, preventing spending on popular projects, thereby weakening support for the government. And those who upheld the Confucian ideals of decorum and restraint might attack the institution of kisaeng and the government bureaucracy as decadent and hypocritical. On the other hand, there were those who supported it because it helped to legitimize the government by centralizing the arts and monopolizing cultural symbols of national unity. There were also strong supporters of the institution who claimed that it assisted the government in controlling the army, especially those troops assigned farthest away from the capital. Although there were many attempts to disband the kisaeng, it is important to note that the institution was preserved, through great variations in government policy, for the entire 500 years of the last dynasty.

III. Structure of Sijo

The sijo (a three-line form) originally referred to popular tunes and the somewhat less ephemeral seasonal songs in the late period of the Koryo Dynasty (918–1382). In the early part of the Chosun Dynasty (1392–1910) it referred to a literary genre that was accepted among both the governing class and the populace. This genre had been formed and passed on orally until the invention of the Korean alphabet (hangul) in 1446. Once written Korean was available, the inherent quality of the sijo form made it possible to be taken up by a wide range of social groups.

There is a natural affinity between the structure of the sijo and the structure of much personal expression. The form of the sijo provided a means for the governing-class literati to report on their political situation (in the first two lines) and to moralize about it (in the last line). Their poems, though intended as lyrical and personal, eventually became rigidly conventional in theme and diction. When used by the kisaeng, other inherent capacities of the form were realized. The form itself encouraged construction of a logical and empirical base from which one might securely leap into daring, interpretive, and intimate comments. One might even consider the sijo as a social crib for witty conversation. This aspect of the sijo invited the kisaeng, given their formal social entertaining, to participate actively and excel as poets.

In Korean, the three lines of the sijo are written in phrase groupings of specified numbers of syllables separated by pauses of varying strengths.[5] The usual sizes of the phrase groups and the strengths of pauses are indicated in the diagram below. Note that the unbracketed numbers indicate how many syllables are in that phrase group. The bracketed numbers indicate the strength of that pause; the higher the number the longer the pause.

Phrase: 3 [pause: 1]   4 [2]   3 or 4 [1]   4 [3]
         3 [1]   4 [2]   3 or 4 [1]   4 [4]
         3 [2]   5 [1 or 2]   4 [2]   3

In translating, an attempt was made to establish an abstract structure for the English versions that would allow for an effective relationship between word groups and pauses. Thus the first Korean line became a rudimentary English stanza of two lines, a non-rhyming couplet that is marked off by syntactic unity. The second Korean line break, which carries the heaviest pause, is embodied in the English abstract structure by a pronounced separation into quatrain and final couplet (neither of which is required to rhyme), which are delineated by syntactic boundaries The following diagram is the result of an attempt to create an appropriate English structure for translating the sijo:

```
Phrase [pause: 1/2 or 0]   Phrase [pause: 1]
Phrase [pause: 1/2 or 0]   Phrase [pause: 2]
Phrase [pause: 1/2 or 0]   Phrase [pause: 1]
Phrase [pause: 1/2 or 0]   Phrase [pause: 4]

Phrase [pause: 1/2 or 0]   Phrase [pause: 1 or 2]
Phrase [pause: 1/2 or 0]   Phrase
```

Keeping in mind that this is an abstract structure, expressive variation from this model has been allowed, indeed, sought in the actual translations. This structure itself varies in a number of ways from the Korean version, but the use of a different language demands structural change. If, for example, the English model were simply left in a three-line form, with an extra space, say, between the second and third lines, the sense of reflection, commentary, conclusion, or ironic relation that is possible in the third line of the Korean would be greatly attenuated for the third line of the English version. Two lines of a Korean sijo can establish a much greater texture of thought, feeling, and poetic experience than the usual two lines of English verse. The English version needs more room. The shifting of the English version into a mixture of couplet and quatrain stanzas allows a fidelity to the capacities of the Korean form. The final English stanza can function as the final Korean line does, much in the manner of a concluding couplet to a sonnet.

NOTES

1. Kim Ok Kil, et al. *Hankuk Yosongsa* [*A History of Korean Women*], (Seoul: Eewha Women's University Press, 1977), 529.

2. Kim, 518.

3. Chang Sa-hun, "Women Entertainers of the Yi Dynasty" [*Women of the Yi Dynasty*], ed. Young-hai Park (Seoul: Sookmyung Women's University Press, 1986), 262.

4. Kim, 520.

5. Richard Rutt, *An Introduction to the Sijo, Transactions of the Korea Branch of the Royal Asiatic Society.* Vol. xxxiv (Seoul, 1958).

Hwang Jini

Ah, What Have I Done?

Ah, what have I done—as though I didn't
know my feelings would remain.
I would not add the few
words that would keep him.

I want to understand the joy
I felt as I was letting him go.

어져 내일이야 그릴줄을 모로 두 냐
이시라 ᄒ더면 가랴마ᄂ 제 구트여
보내고 그리ᄂ 정은 나도 몰라 ᄒ노라

황진이

Hwang Jini

At Cold Solstice

At cold solstice I cut
the night, take its long waist
to my quilted bed,
curl up the dark under

broideries of spring, to wait
a night spread out again for you.

동지돌 기나긴 밤을 한 허리를 버혀내여
춘풍 니블아레 서리서리 너헛다가
어론님 오신날 밤이여든 구뷔구뷔 퍼리라

황진이

Hwang Jini

Blue Stream

Blue stream, don't show off your speed
running down my green mountain.
Once you reach the wide blue sea,
no easy way leads back.

Moonlight now fills my valley;
slow yourself, rest, then go.

청산니 백계수야 수이 감을 쟈랑마라
일도창해 ᄒ면 도라오기 어려오니
명월이 만공산ᄒ니 수여간들 엇더리

황진이

Hwang Jini

I Have a Will

I have a will like a blue mountain;
his love for me is a green running stream.
Shall a blue mountain change
with the rushing of green waters?

He will not forget this blue mountain;
his green cries resound as he goes.

청산은 내 쑷이오 녹수는 님의 정이
녹수 흘너간들 청산이야 변홀손가
녹수도 청산을 뭇니져 우러예어 가는고

황진이

Hwang Jini

Old Mountain

Old mountain, here you are still,
but these are not the same waters:
they have not begun to age,
having flowed on each day, each night.

My lover has been pure as water,
coming to me, going away.

산은 녯산이로되 물은 녯물 안이로다
주야에 흘은이 녯물리 이실쏜야
인걸도 물과 굿도다 가고 안이 오느미라

황진이

Hwang Jini

When Ever Did I?

When ever did I break trust? When
did I ever break words to you? Dark
so deep the risen moon was drowned,
and you would not bestow a sign.

Dead leaves are shaken by spring winds,
yet I have nothing now to do with sound.

내 언제 무신ㅎ여 님을 언제 소겻관듸
월심삼경에 온 뜻이 전혀업늬
춘풍에 지는 님소릐야 낸들 어이 ㅎ리오

황진이

Im Je

Are You Napping?

Are you napping or just hiding, lying
still in this gully of wild blue grass?
Where is the high color of your face?
Only white bones lie here.

I hold a cup you can never fill,
that I cannot raise to my sorrow.

Note: This is the only poem written by a male poet (1549–1587) in this collection.
It is included because his poem is a tribute to Hwang Jini.

청초 우거진 골에 자는다 누엇는다

홍안을 어듸 두고 백골만 무쳣는이

잔자바 권흐리 업스니 그를 슬허 흐노라

임제

Chinok

Iron, We Were Told

Iron, we were told; iron had arrived again.
Sure, I remembered brittle pig iron,
but your close, cold surface told me iron
again that was hammered and annealed.

This time I will use a furnace of earth, bellows
of such breath you will not withstand the fire.

철이 철이라커 놀 섭철만 너겨써니
이제야 보아흐니 정철일시 분명흐다
내게 골블무 잇던니 뇌겨 블가 흐노라

진옥

Chongum

As Evening Entered

As evening entered our mountain town
a faint howl followed from a distance.
I opened my door of woven branches. One
cold light of the sky fell on me.

Howl, dog, the moon sleeps
stretched over the empty mountainside.

산촌에 밤이 드니 먼뒷 기 즈져온다
사리를 열고 보니 하늘이 차고 달이로다
뎌 기야 공산 줌든 달을 즈져 무슴 ᄒ리요

종음

Why Freeze?

Why freeze to sleep?
What good are dreams of frost?
Having no bed with quilted birds,
must I sleep in the cold?

Today, I felt the freezing rain.
Tonight, I'll have a sleep that thaws.

어이 얼어 잘이 므스 일 얼어 잘이
원앙침 비취금을 어듸 두고 얼어 자리
오늘은 춘비 맛자신이 녹아 잘까 ᄒ노라

한우

Hoeyon

In Fall, When the Moon

In fall, when the moon visits my garden,
each chrysanthemum contends for the light.
But the scented plum tree waits
for memory within a branch to blossom.

From under the deep coming frost
you alone will emerge unchanged.

추월이 만정한데 국화는 유의로다
향매화 일지심은 날 못잊어 피는구나
아마도 오상고절은 너뿐인가 하노라

회연

Under the Cold, Pine Arbor Moon

Under the cold, pine arbor moon,
small waves lap the Seacoast Tower.
Some gulls land, others take off
—to fly away and back.

My love departs,
not to return.

한송정 둘 붉은 밤의 경포대예 물썰 잔제
유신호 백구는 오락가락 ㅎ 것만은
엇덧타 우리의 왕손은 가고 안이 오 는이

홍장

Hongnang

I Chose This Branch

I chose this branch of mountain willow,
had it cut and carried to your hand.
Bury it under your bedroom window,
let it grow in shadow, and see

a new leaf come from midnight rains:
in that new leaf me.

뫼ㅅ버들 갈히 것거 보내노라 님의손디
자시는 창밧긔 심거두고 보쇼셔
밤비예 새닙 곳 나거든 날인가도 너기쇼셔

홍낭

The Large Beak Finches

The large beak finches have flown away,
and the sky lines of wild geese have ended.
Here in exile, behind ocean walls,
only a dream is allowed to exist.

I regret this passage of dream
will not have left any traces.

청조도 날아가고 홍안이 그치었다
수성적소에 다만 한 꿈뿐이로다
꿈길이 자취 없으니 그를 설워하노라

임니월

Imniwol

We Tied His Horse

We tied his horse to the woven gate,
unclasped our hands.
What was it I cried for
with crystalline tears, jade white face?

Perhaps he was already the one
I will not be forgetting.

시문에 말을 매고 임과 분수할 제
옥안주루가 눌로하여 흘렀는고
아마도 못 잊을손 임이신가 하노라

임니월

At Some Thoughts

At some thoughts of him
my eyes can still cry.
That fall the wild geese flew so far south
they took the sky with them.

Stay just as far away as you can;
time will keep or lead you back.

시시로 생각ᄒ니 눈물이 멋줄이오
북천 상안이 언의새여 도라올고
두어라 연분 미진ᄒ면 다시 볼가 ᄒ노라

강강월

Kang Gangwol

Late One Night

Late one night, alone, unsleeping,
I heard the wild geese cry.
Raising more wick to flame,
I continued my turning.

Then low, heavy sounds of rain
made me feel dimmer, farther away.

기러기 우는밤에 닉홀노 좀이업셔
잔등 도도혀고 전전불상 ᄒ 눈츠에
창밧게 굵은 비소리에 더욱 망연ᄒ여라

강강월

Kang Gangwol

While Journeying

While journeying a thousand miles,
I met him—we touched and parted.
Now that I dream so far again,
my beloved will stay.

Each morning, I awake,
my vision spilling.

천리에 만나다가 천리에 이별 한 니
천리 꿈속에 님 보거고나
꿈씨야 다시금 생각 한 니 눈물겨워 한 노라

강강월

Keju

Let My Cassia Boat

Let my cassia boat be tied:
this bank has green willows and red grass;
this is the time of the sun leaving
the mountain and river many come to pass.

When a spring wind touches me,
alone, I'll take my boat across.

녹양 홍료변에 계주를 느저 매고
일모 강산에 건널 이 하도 할샤
어즈버 순풍을 만나거든 혼자 건너 가리라

계주

Kuji

My Boat, Cut

My boat, cut from tallest pine,
was sent floating down the Tae-dong
until I held fast to him
by the deep-root willow.

And now, you, mindless thing, call me
back into dark rip tides.

장송으로 비를 무어 대동강에 씌워 두고
유일지 휘여다가 굿이굿이 미얏는듸
어듸셔 망녕엣 거슨 소혜 들라 ᄒ 는이

구지

Kumhong

Wild Geese Sang

Wild geese sang across a thin jade sky;
I opened my window, leaned out to see
—moonlit snow had so filled my garden,
light seemed to reach wherever he might be.

This vision took such deep root
its cold glimmers faded within me.

벽천홍안성에 창을 열고 늬다보니
설월이 만정ᄒᆞ여 님의 곳 빗취려니
아마도 심중한전수는 나쓴인가 ᄒᆞ노라

금홍

Who Caught You?

Who caught you, fish, then set you free
within my garden pond?
Which clear northern sea did you leave
for these small waters?

Once here, with no way to flee,
you and I are the same.

압못세 든 고기들아 뉘라셔 너를 모라다가 넉커늘
든다
북해 청소를 어듸 두고 이못세 와 든다
들고도 못나는 정은 네오니오 다르랴

궁녀

Kyerang

Petals Rained

Petals rained from the pear trees
as I cried within my arms to him.
Now that the fall wind takes the leaf,
does he keep me a place within?

My dreams range the miles to him
and return weary of travel.

이화우 훗색릴제 울며 잡고 이별흔 님
추풍낙엽에 저도 날 싱각는가
천리에 외로온 꿈만 오락가락 ㅎ노매

계량

Kyesom

Just When

Just when did my green age go
and this gray overtake me?
Had I but known what time
the changing was to be . . .

But being in the way does not block it;
knowing the way would have led me to mourn.

청춘은 언제 가며 백발은 언제 온고
오고 ㄱ는 길을 아돗던들 막을 거슬
알고도 못 막는 길히니 그를 슬허 ㅎ노라

계섬

Maehwa

As I Tossed

As I tossed deeply into night, turned
into its last sleepless region,
the heavy clattering-bell rains came
to sound the wound he left inside me.

Someone tell him my wanderings,
the night-worn lines across my face.

심야 오경토록 잠못일워 전전헐졔
구즌비 문령성이 상사로 단장이라
뉘라셔 이 행색 글려다가 님의 압헤

매화

Maehwa

I Would Have To

I would have to take each and every
detail of my constant thoughts of him
and send them through the silk curtain
across the moonlit window of his room

to have a chance that he imagine
I have a longing that will not spare him.

심중에 무한사을 세세히 옴겨다가
월사창 금수장에 님 계신곳 전ㅎ고져
그제야 알들이 글리는줄 짐작이나

매화

Maehwa

My Thoughts of Him

My thoughts of him are muscle and bone,
for he loved me with no flesh to spare.
One moment's longing for another touch
of him cuts through my belly.

How then shall I live
through these days after days?

살뜰한 내 마음과 알뜰한 임의 정을
일시 상봉 그리워도 단장 심회이거늘
하물며 몇몇 날을 이래도록

매화

Maehwa

To This Old Stump

To this old stump of a plum tree
springtime does return.
Each time, this branch has flowered;
maybe it will once more.

Spring snow bewilders the sky;
there may or may not be a new flower.

매화 녯등걸에 봄졀이 도라오니
녯퓌던 가지에 픠염즉도 ㅎ다마ㄴ
춘셜이 난분분ㅎ니 필 동말동 ㅎ여라

매화

Maehwa

What Blight

What blight is this eating into my desire
for a man, for whose vows I pledged my life?
There are times when thinking on my
thinking of him lets me read the signs.

Not a word to him—who is he
to know what lies in my far sight?

평생에 밋을 님을 글려 무삼 병들손가
시시로 상사심은 지기ᄒ는 타시로다
두어라 알들헌 이 심정을 님이 어이

매화

Munhyang

All Right Then

All right then, but don't say those words. If you
no longer look on me, why must you keep talking?
If heaven looked down on you alone,
then should you talk as though chosen.

We are all, all from heaven;
there is a love sent for me.

오냐 말아니짜나 실커니 아니 말랴
하늘아래 너뿐이면 아마 내야 호려니와
하늘이 다 삼겻스니 날 꾈인들 업스랴

문향

Myongok

Don't Tell Me the Face

Don't tell me the face I have now
would have been traced for its beauty.
Sad thoughts become a visible thread
that winds itself until knotted.

Effort will not straighten it,
seeking will not find the end.

예라 이리 하면 이 얼굴을 기럿으랴
수심이 실이 되어 굽이굽이 맺혀 있어
아모리 풀으려 하여도 끝간 데를 몰래라.

명옥

Myongok

A Lover That Shows

A lover that shows himself only
in a dream I would call a liar.
But outside of dream I cannot
show myself my own desire.

You there, do not call yourself
a dream, just show yourself to me.

꿈에 뵈는 님아 신의업다 ㅎ 것마는
분분이 그리올졔 꿈아니면 어이보리
져 님아 꿈이라 말고 ㅈ로ㅈ로 뵈시쇼

명옥

Okson

They Say

They say love is good for one,
that it shows best in parting.
It took my life to see the first
time can mean never again.

They say if you take love,
you must give pain.

뉘라서 정 좋다고 하던고 이별에도 인정인가
평생에 처음이요 다시 못 볼 임이로다
아마도 정 주고 병 얻기는 나뿐인가

옥선

Pudong

If You

If you were Yi-doryong,
would I be your Chun-hyang?
They shared one mind, two bodies,
envied no one, no, not even the eternal.

Their mind reflected
light from clear skies.

Note: Yi-doryong and Chun-hyang are triumphant lovers in Korean folklore.

춘향이 네로더냐 이 도령 그 뉘러니
양인일심이 만겁인들 부럴소냐
아마도 이 마음 비치기는 명천인가 하노라

부동

Songdaechun

A Butterfly from Seoul

A butterfly from Seoul breezed through
our Bed of a Hundred Flowers,
quivered in the Moon Gazebo,
sat poised on the Pavilion of Pines.

But seeing the first spring blossom
of plum, he found no gesture for his joy.

한양서 떠 온 나비 백화총에 들거구나
은하월에 잠깐 쉬어 송대에 올라 앉아
이따금 매화춘색에 흥을 겨워하노라

송대천

Songi

Everything You Do

Everything you do, everything
you don't do, deceives.
When I love, I make you
my enemy.

But the words you spoke
keep themselves within me.

이리ㅎ여 날 속이고 져리ㅎ여 날 속이니
원슈이 님을 이졈즉도 ㅎ다마ᄂ
전전에 언약이 즁ㅎ니 못이즐가 ㅎ노라

송이

Songi

Hush, Rooster

Hush, rooster—boasting as though
you were the first to wake!
No great man is trapped within,
awaiting your voice to unlock the gate.

The one morning my man is still with me
—yet, you yell of escape.

Note: The "great man" in line three refers to Maengsang-kun, a well-remembered
Chinese Minister of State. Fleeing at night from the Chin toward the Cheh territo-
ries, he is said to have passed through a crucial city gate, not scheduled to open till
dawn, by having his companion fake a cock's crow.

닭아 우지마라 일 우노라 즈랑마라

반야진관에 맹상군이 아니로다

오늘은 님오신 날이니 아니 운들 엇더리

송이

Songi

I Sit Up

I sit up alone tonight
while others I know are sleeping.
I cannot choose on which side to lie
to think of my beloved or his lover.

Since my beloved loves another,
I will not meet his thoughts.

남은 자는 밤에 내 어이 홀로 앉아
전전 불매하고 임 둔 임을 생각는고
그 임도 임 둔 임이니 생각할 줄이 있으랴

송이

Songi

Love Is Not

Love is not for every lover,
nor sadness for every parting.
My first became a love
I was not to feel again.

If we are yet to meet,
then it must be.

스랑인들 님마다 ᄒ며 이별인들 다 셜우랴
평생에 처음이요 다시 못 볼 님이로다
이 후에 다시 만나면 연분인가 ᄒ노라.

송이

Songi

The River of Stars

The river of stars must have flooded
over your bridge of magpies and crows
for you, who guide a bull of heaven,
not to know how to cross to my side.

I am a weaver who can only wait
with a weaver's heart.

은하에 물이 진이 오작교에 쓰닷말가
쇼 잇슨 선랑이 못건너 가닷말가
직녀의 촌만흔 간장이 다 긋츨가 ㅎ노라

송이

Songi

So, You Can Tell

So, you can tell I'm a pine,
but what kind do you take me for?
I have grown tall and wide
overlooking this precipice.

And you, prentice, from below the timber
road, wish a pruning blade on me.

솔이 솔이라 흔이 므슨 솔만 넉이는다
천심절벽에 낙낙장송 내 긔로라
길알에 초동의 졉낫시야 걸어볼쭐 잇시랴

송이

Songi

When a Butterfly Sees a Flower

When a butterfly sees a flower,
it must dance, the flower smile.
Whenever they come into season,
this is love to them.

Our love too has a season
which must not come again.

곳 보고 춤추는 나뷔와 나뷔 보고 당싯 웃는 곳과
져 들의 ᄉ랑은 절절이 오건마는
엇더틋 우리의 ᄉ랑은 가고 아니 오느니

송이

Songi

Our Love Is Not

Our love is not for you to give
nor others' for you to crave.
Take care, you take
our love with you.

For such love, I have lived;
for such a life, I will love.

내사랑 남 주지 말고 눔의 사랑을 탐치 마소
울이의 두 사랑에 잡사랑 행여 섯낄쎄라
평생에 이 사랑 가지고 백년동락 ᄒ리라

송이

Tabok

At the Last Waste of Dark

At the last waste of dark,
the North Dipper declining,
I knew I couldn't earn the vow he'd given
to meet on one of the Ten Blessed Isles.

One jealous evening—what does it matter?
Let him have companions he likes.

북두성 기울어지고 경오점 즈자간다
십주가기는 허랑타 ᄒ리로다
두어라 번우ᄒ 님이니 새와 무슴 ᄒ리오

타복

Anonymous

An Anchor Lifts

An anchor lifts, a ship is leaving;
he goes this time, when to return.
Far over the sea's vast waverings
one can see a going as return.

But at the sound of that anchor lifting,
the night could hear her insides turn.

닷쓰쟈 비쎠나가니 이졔 가면 언졔 오리
만경창파에 가는듯 단녀옴셰
밤중만 지국총 소릐에 이긋눈듯 ㅎ여라

무명인

Anonymous

Before They Cross

Before they cross this mountain ridge,
the wind, even the clouds, must rest.
Before these heights, sea hawk and cliff hawk
must pause, then soar over.

But tell me he is on the other side,
and I will yield no pause, no rest.

바람도 쉬어 넘고 구름이라도 쉬어 넘는 고개
산진수진이라도 쉬어 넘는 고봉 장성령 고개
그 너머 임이 왔다 하면 나는 한번도 아니 쉬어
    넘으리라.

                      무명인

Anonymous

The Black Crow

The black crow does not paint itself,
nor does the crane turn itself white.
From time past, from their sky-given
birth, black and white have been.

Here I am. My lover sees me.
Yet he talks of black and white.

가마귀 칠ᄒᆞ여 검우며 ᄒᆡ오리 늙어 희냐
천성혹백이 네붓터 잇건마ᄂᆞᆫ
엇디톤 날 보신 님은 검다 희다 ᄒᆞᄂᆞᆫ고

무명인

Anonymous

If Tears Were Pearls

If tears were pearls, I would have
held mine back, those ten waited years,
to build a palace of pearl
to have him sit within.

There there is nothing now,
that is my new sorrow.

눈물이 진주라면 흐르지 않게 싸두었다
십년후 오신님에 앉히련만
흔적이 이내 없으니 그를 설어 하노라.

무명인

Anonymous

If Rain

If rain can come,
why can't he?
If clouds can go,
why can't I?

When he and I are rain and clouds,
then shall we know coming and going.

비는 오신다마는 임은 어이 못 오시노
구름은 간다마는 나는 어이 못 가는고
우리도 언제 구름 비 되어 오락가락 하리오.

무명인

Anonymous

So, What Is This Love?

So, what is this love?
Is it round or flat;
is it long or short enough to be
paced off or laid beside a ruler?

Some say it lasts as long as it lessens;
mine breaks to a sharp edge within me.

ᄉ랑이 엇더터니 두렷더냐 넙엿더냐
기더냐 쟈르더냐 발을러냐 자힐러냐
지멸이 긴 줄은 모로되 애 그츨만 ᄒ더라

　　　　　　　　　　무명인

Anonymous

Stop

Stop blowing yourself, wind,
over the snow of my moonlit garden.
You cannot become the sound
of his shoes pushing through the snow.

You can't bring what has gone;
let me long, let me listen.

설월이 만정한데 바람아 불지 마라
예부셩 아닌 줄을 판연히 알건마는
그립고 아쉬운 마음에 행여 긴가 하노라.

무명인

Anonymous

Were There Two

Were there two lives for us,
you would become me, and I you.
Becoming me, you would still desire
me and so tear yourself as I tore you.

Only turn yourself around to see all
my life, to know all my pain.

우리 둘이 후생ᄒ야 네 나되고 내 너되야
내 너 글여 굿든 에를 너도 날 글여 굿처 보면
이생에 내 셜워ᄒ든줄을 너도 알까 ᄒ노라

무명인

Anonymous

What Struck Me

What struck me from the sound
of rain on Lotus Flower Pond
to wake me from the dream
that was to bring my lover?

The leaves held glassy beads,
as though tears rose from green.

연못싀 비 오ᄂ 소릐 긔 무어시 놀납관ᄃᆡ
님 보라 가던 ᄭᅮᆷ이 못 보고 ᄭᅦ돗던고
닙 우희 구슬만 담겨 눈물 듯듯 ᄒ더라.

무명인

Acknowledgments

Our thanks go to Korean women poets and writers, too numerous to name here, who led us to the kisaeng; to Suh Younguen, inspirational in this regard, who was also instrumental in obtaining generous grants from the Korean Culture and Arts Foundation for the project; to Park Sangun, of the Foundation, for his patient support during our search for the right publisher; and to Mun Chunghi, who helped us compile the poems of this book.

We owe special thanks to Allen Mandelbaum and Christopher Ricks for their kindness in reading the manuscript and suggesting a great many improvements.

We wish to thank the editors of the following journals, where some of these translations first appeared: *Asian Pacific American Journal*; *The Beloit Poetry Journal*; *The Chicago Review*; *Grand Street*; *The Ledge*; *Lift*; *New England Review/Bread Loaf Quarterly*; *Pequod*; *Poetry East*; and *TriQuarterly*.

Finally, we thank Sam Hamill and our editors, Steve Huff and Thom Ward, whose appreciation of the poems made the book possible.

About the Translators

Constantine Contogenis has published in several journals and has received poetry fellowships from the Edward Albee, Tyrone Guthrie, Ragdale, and Helen Wurlitzer Foundations. He lives in New York City.

Wolhee Choe, also of New York City, is Professor of English at Polytechnic University, and is the author or translator of numerous books on poetry, painting, and poetics.

BOA EDITIONS, LTD.
NEW AMERICAN TRANSLATIONS SERIES

Vol. 1   *Illuminations*
         Poems by Arthur Rimbaud
         Translated by Bertrand Mathieu with Foreword by Henry Miller

Vol. 2   *Exaltation of Light*
         Poems by Homero Aridjis
         Translated by Eliot Weinberger

Vol. 3   *The Whale and Other Uncollected Translations*
         Richard Wilbur

Vol. 4   *Beings and Things on Their Own*
         Poems by Katerina Anghelaki-Rooke
         Translated by the Author in Collaboration with Jackie Willcox

Vol. 5   *Anne Hébert: Selected Poems*
         Translated by A. Poulin, Jr.

Vol. 6   *Yannis Ritsos: Selected Poems 1938–1988*
         Edited and Translated by Kimon Friar and Kostas Myrsiades

Vol. 7   *The Flowers of Evil and Paris Spleen*
         Poems by Charles Baudelaire
         Translated by William H. Crosby

Vol. 8   *A Season in Hell and Illuminations*
         Poems by Arthur Rimbaud
         Translated by Bertrand Mathieu

Vol. 9   *Day Has No Equal but Night*
         Poems by Anne Hébert
         Translated by A. Poulin, Jr.

Vol. 10 *Songs of the Kisaeng*
         Courtesan Poetry of the Last Korean Dynasty
         Translated by Constantine Contogenis and Wolhee Choe